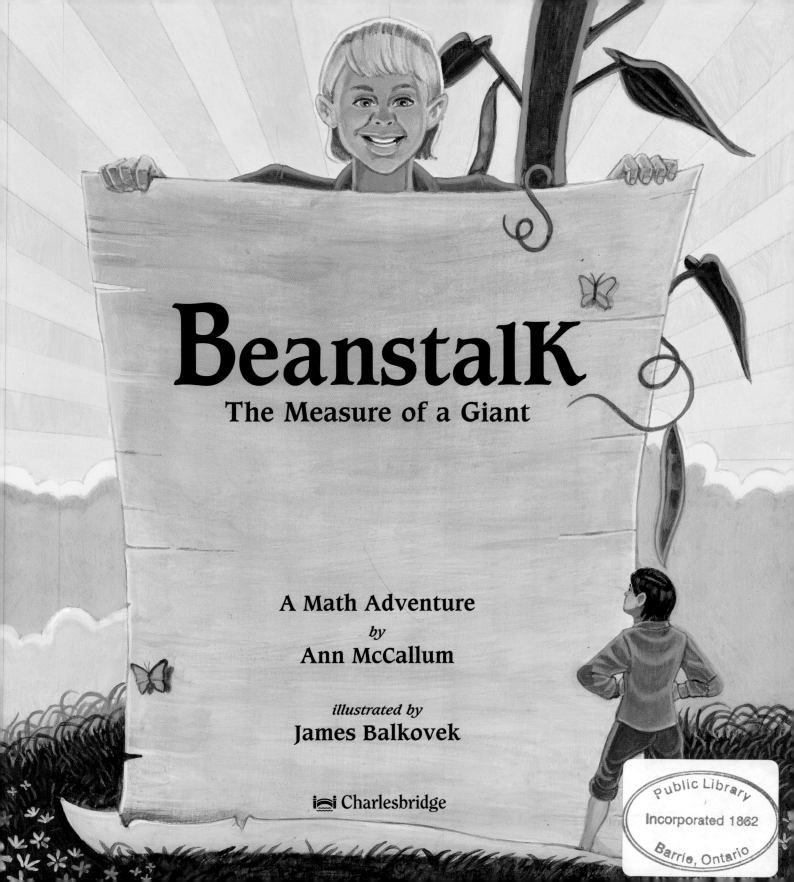

BeanstalK

The Measure of a Giant

A Math Adventure
by
Ann McCallum

illustrated by
James Balkovek

ꔹ Charlesbridge

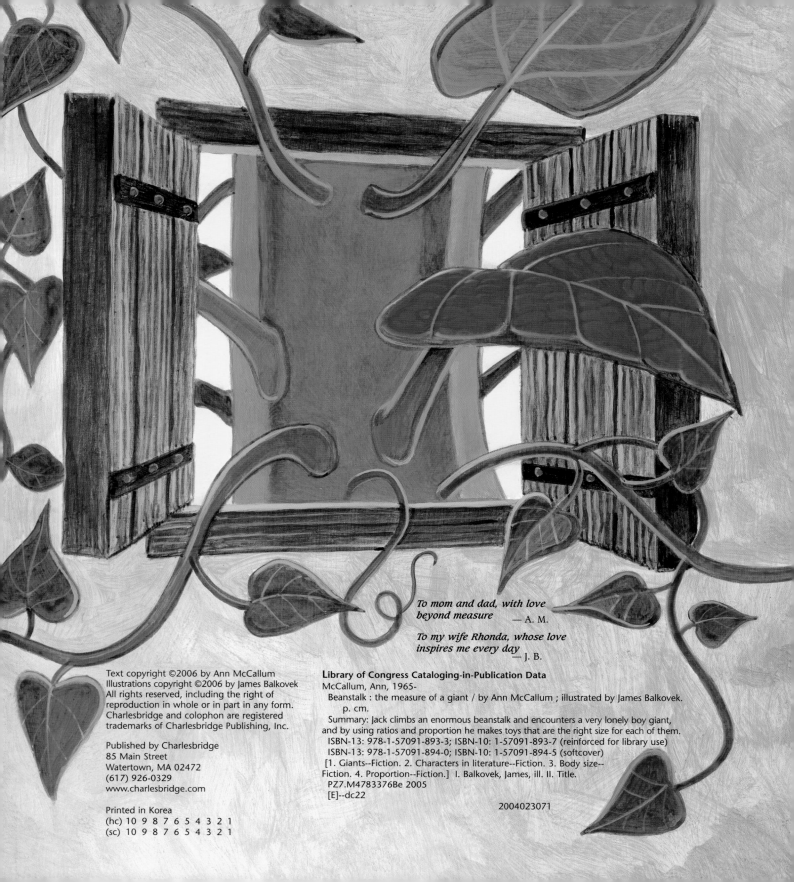

*To mom and dad, with love
beyond measure*
— A. M.

*To my wife Rhonda, whose love
inspires me every day*
— J. B.

Text copyright ©2006 by Ann McCallum
Illustrations copyright ©2006 by James Balkovek
All rights reserved, including the right of
reproduction in whole or in part in any form.
Charlesbridge and colophon are registered
trademarks of Charlesbridge Publishing, Inc.

Published by Charlesbridge
85 Main Street
Watertown, MA 02472
(617) 926-0329
www.charlesbridge.com

Printed in Korea
(hc) 10 9 8 7 6 5 4 3 2 1
(sc) 10 9 8 7 6 5 4 3 2 1

Library of Congress Cataloging-in-Publication Data
McCallum, Ann, 1965-
  Beanstalk : the measure of a giant / by Ann McCallum ; illustrated by James Balkovek.
     p. cm.
  Summary: Jack climbs an enormous beanstalk and encounters a very lonely boy giant,
and by using ratios and proportion he makes toys that are the right size for each of them.
  ISBN-13: 978-1-57091-893-3; ISBN-10: 1-57091-893-7 (reinforced for library use)
  ISBN-13: 978-1-57091-894-0; ISBN-10: 1-57091-894-5 (softcover)
 [1. Giants--Fiction. 2. Characters in literature--Fiction. 3. Body size--
Fiction. 4. Proportion--Fiction.] I. Balkovek, James, ill. II. Title.
PZ7.M4783376Be 2005
[E]--dc22
                                           2004023071

"What's that?" Jack woke up to a strange sound outside his window. All of a sudden, his shutters burst open and a tangle of leaves filled his room.

3

Jack rushed outside. An enormous beanstalk towered over the house. "Did this grow from those beans I got?" asked Jack.

"Must have!" his mother replied. "With these big beans, we won't go hungry."

"Look how it reaches right up to the sky," Jack said, stepping onto a huge leaf. "I'm going to see where it goes."

"Be careful, Jack!" his mother called after him.

Jack was way up high before he stopped to rest. A flock of birds flew past him.

"Look how high up I am!" he said. "From up here my house looks tiny. I can cover the whole village with my hand."

Jack climbed even higher. He was near the top when he felt a splash. He looked up, but instead of rain clouds he saw a huge boy crying.

The boy wiped his eyes and sniffed, "Fee fi foe foy, I smell the scent of a human boy."

"Oh, no," Jack thought, "He is so big he must be a giant."

Jack ducked behind a leaf and watched the giant boy. After a minute, Jack said right out loud, "He may be big, but he seems like any other kid."

The giant stopped crying. "Who's there?" he asked.

Jack stepped out into the open and said, "Hi. I'm Jack. What's the matter?"

"I don't have any friends," the giant boy said.

"Aren't there any kids around here your age and umm . . . size?" asked Jack.

The giant boy shook his head from side to side.

"I'll be your friend," Jack offered.

"Okay," the giant boy smiled and sat down so he was closer to Jack's size. "My name's Ray," he said.

9

"So, what games do you like to play?" asked Jack.

"I like hoopball," Ray said.

"Hoopball is the best!" Jack agreed. "Let's play."

Ray got his ball. It was almost as big as Jack.

"I think we have a problem," Jack said.

Ray nodded, "I'll be right back."
He returned a few minutes
later with a smaller ball.

"This is better," said Jack.
"Where's the hoop?"

Ray pointed up.

Jack whistled. "No one my size
can shoot a ball that high.
I need a lower hoop."

"We can't play hoopball
with two different hoops,"
Ray said.

"We can just shoot hoops. Each time we get the ball in the hoop, we get a letter. The first one with enough letters to spell **b-e-a-n-s-t-a-l-k** wins," Jack said. "For the game to be fair though, I need a hoop that's as high for me as your hoop is for you."

"Well, I'm 20 feet tall," Ray said.

"Whew," said Jack. "How high is your hoop?"

"It's 60 feet high," Ray answered.

"Your hoop is three times your height," Jack said. "So my hoop has to be three times my height, and I'm 48 inches tall."

"That's 4 feet." Ray said. He got a measuring tape and measured. Then he bent a branch 12 feet from the ground into a circle.

"Great!" said Jack.

13

After a few games of b-e-a-n-s-t-a-l-k, Jack heard a strange noise like thunder. "What's that?" he asked.

"Oh, that's my stomach rumbling," Ray said. "It's time for lunch." Ray went to his house and came back with a plate of food.

Jack ate a cracker that was as big as a dinner plate. "So what's it like up here?"

"It's pretty good," Ray said. "What's it like down there?"

The sun sank
lower in the sky
as the boys told
each other about
their homes. Then
Ray said, "Let's
play shadows."

"I look as big as you!"
Jack said, looking at his
elongated shadow.

"But I'm still bigger," Ray
said as his shadow stretched
toward the horizon. They
made shadow shapes until it
was time for Jack to go home.

"You'll never guess what I did today!" Jack said when he got home. He told his mother all about Ray. "Tomorrow, I want to show him how to play checkers."

"You and the giant playing checkers?" his mother chuckled. "To him, a checker would be no bigger than a bean."

"Hmm . . . I'll make giant-sized checkers," said Jack.

"How big should I make them?" Jack drew a picture of himself and Ray. "I'm 4 feet tall and Ray is 20 feet tall.

"That's five times bigger, so I'll make Ray's checkerboard 5 times the size of mine."

5
TIMES
AS
TALL

RAY
20 ft.

ME
4 ft.

Jack found his checkerboard, measured it, and multiplied by five.

On a big sheet of paper, he drew seven parallel lines. Then, to make squares, he drew seven perpendicular lines. He painted the squares red and black.

Then he sawed a log into checkers $7\frac{1}{2}$ inches across.

He painted them red and black, too.

The next day, Jack climbed the beanstalk and knocked on Ray's door. The giant who opened it looked down and smiled. "Hello," she said.

"I have a present for Ray!" He gave her the game.

"How nice," she replied. "I'm Ray's mother. I'll take you to his room."

Jack ran to keep up with her. "I feel like I've shrunk," he said as he took a shortcut under a table.

Jack was surprised by how much Ray's room was like his room. He set up the checkerboard and explained how to play.

"This is fun," Ray said after winning a game. They played for most of the morning.

Then Jack said, "Let's have lunch at my house."

"Okay!" Ray agreed.

Jack climbed down the
beanstalk. When Ray tried
to climb down, the beanstalk
began to bend.

"It isn't strong enough
to hold me," Ray said.

21

"Maybe we can make a ladder to the ground," Jack said.

Ray got some rope and asked "How long should we make the ladder?"

"I guess it should be as long as the beanstalk," said Jack. "Do you still have that measuring tape?"

"Sure do," said Ray, and took it out of his pocket.

Ray lowered his measuring tape down the beanstalk. It got caught in the leaves.

"Maybe we can tie a weight to it so it will go through the leaves," Jack said. They tied a rock to the end of the tape but it still got tangled up.

Ray turned to Jack, "What if we tie you to the measuring tape? You could keep it from getting stuck."

23

"I think this is going to work," Jack said as Ray slowly lowered him down.

Looking at the ground below, Jack saw that the sun made everything cast a shadow.

24

"The length of the shadow depends on the height of what's casting the shadow," Jack thought. Suddenly he jerked to a stop.

"Oh no!" Ray called down. "The measuring tape isn't long enough."

"That's okay. Pull me up," Jack said. "I have an idea."

"What's your idea?" Ray asked, after pulling Jack up.

"First I need to measure your shadow." Ray stood up straight while Jack measured.

It was just about noon, so Ray's shadow was only 2 feet long.

"Now I'll compare it to the shadow of the beanstalk."

Jack scurried down the beanstalk as quick
as a mouse. He measured its shadow.

It was 41 feet long.

He scratched a picture in the dirt.
Jack yelled up to Ray, "The beanstalk
is 410 feet tall!"

"How do you know that?"
Ray called back.

"Your shadow was 2 feet long, one-tenth of your height, so the shadow of the beanstalk has to be one-tenth of the beanstalk's height."

2 FT. SHADOW
20 FT TALL

41 FT. SHADOW
? FT TALL

$$\frac{2}{20} = \frac{1}{10}$$

$$\frac{41}{?} = \frac{1}{10}$$

$$41 \times 10 = 410 \, FT$$

Ray made a ladder and climbed down.

"I invited Ray for lunch," Jack said to his mother. "I hope it's okay."

"Sure," his mother said. Then looking at Ray's size, she added, "It's such a nice day, why don't we eat outside?"

She cooked French-fried beans and grilled bean burgers.
As they ate, she said, "You boys get along very well."

"That's because we have a lot in common," Ray said.
"We figured out how to do things together even though
I'm so much taller."

"That's right," said Jack. "To play hoops, we compared
how high Ray's hoop is to how tall Ray is. Then Ray made
a hoop for me that has the same relationship."

"There should be a word for that," Jack's mother said. "A word for the relationship between the size of two things."

"My stuff is the right size for me, just like Ray's stuff is the right size for him. Ray showed me that, so let's call it a 'Ray show.'"

"I like it," Ray said with a huge grin.

From that day on Jack and Ray were best friends (though some people tell a different story) and the relationship between two numbers is still called a "Ray show," but today we spell it *ratio*.

As for the beanstalk, it provided an endless supply of beans for every breakfast, lunch, and dinner. That might be why Jack ate so many meals at Ray's house.

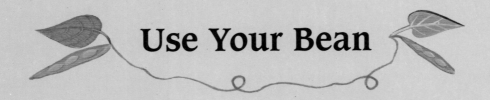

Use Your Bean

Use these activities to help children have more fun with the story and to develop math and language concepts.

1. Ask the children to help you retell the story, explaining each of the challenges Jack and Ray face. Retelling a story helps develop vocabulary and language skills.

2. When Jack makes a checkerboard, he draws parallel and perpendicular lines. Point out parallel lines and perpendicular lines in places such as concrete sidewalks, glass window panes, and mesh window screens. Which of the parallel lines are horizontal (—)? Which are vertical (|)?

3. How big are Jack's checkerboard and checkers? Help the children look for clues in the story. Get a standard checker set and measure it together. How does it compare to Jack's? How big would Jack have to make a checkerboard for a giant who is 50 feet tall?

4. Think of items that are made in sizes: clothing, shoes, bicycles, and so on. Have the children help you measure one of the items. Figure out how big the item would need to be if it were the right size for Ray.

5. Ask the children to think about how Jack might eat dinner at Ray's house. For example, how would he eat giant spaghetti or other giant-sized food? How would he manage a huge fork, knife, and spoon?

6. Ask the children why a shadow changes size. On a sunny day, ask the children to measure the length of your shadow and their own shadows in the morning, at noon, and in the afternoon. Compare a child's shadow to yours. Help the children figure out how the shadows relate to the size of the person casting the shadow.